I0410735

Reindeer Coloring Book for Adults

Reindeer Coloring Book containing various Reindeer designs filled with intricate and stress relieving patterns.

Coloring Books for Adults: Vol 13

by The Coloring Book People

ISBN-13: 978-1541097384

ISBN-10: 1541097386

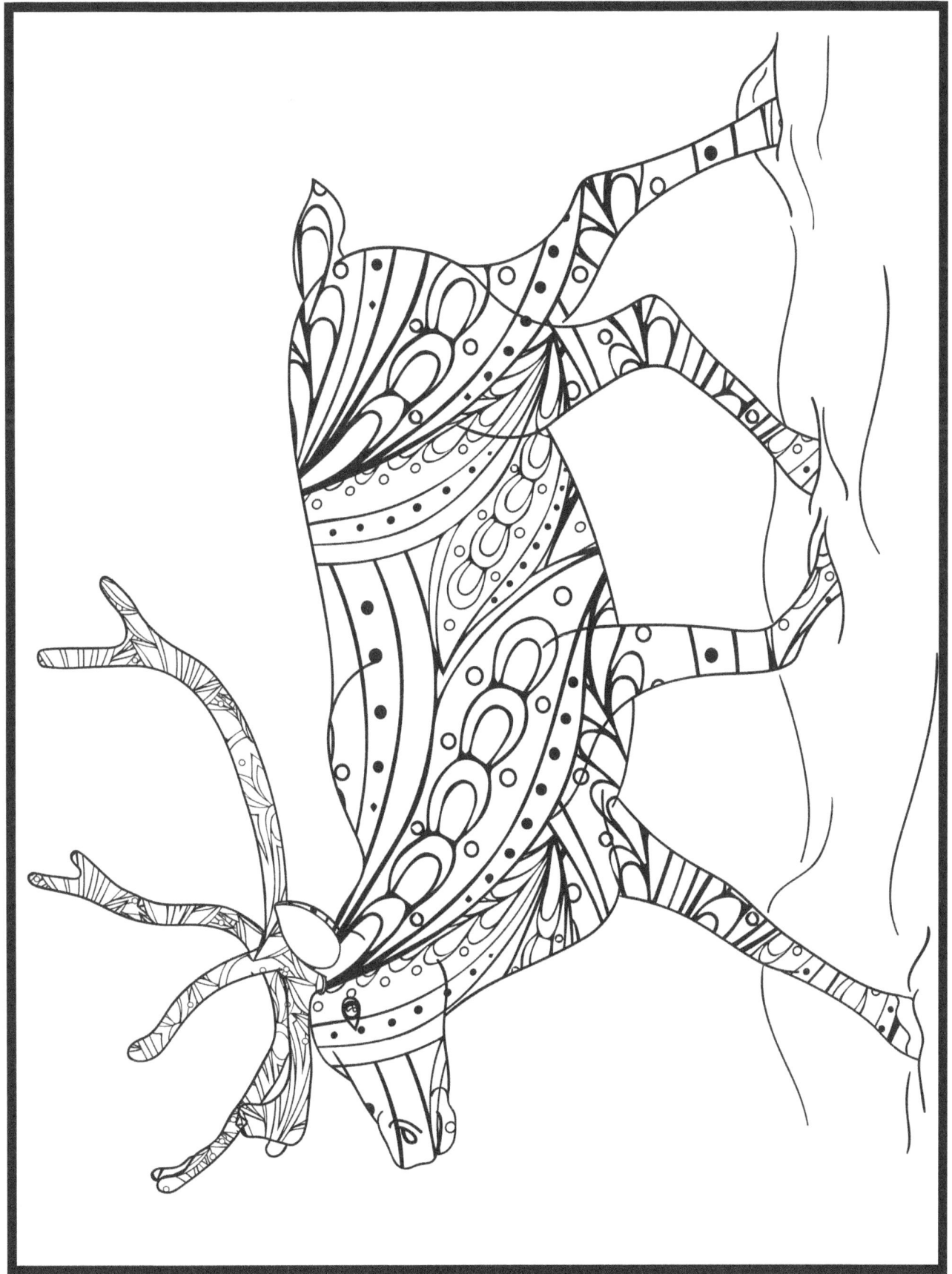

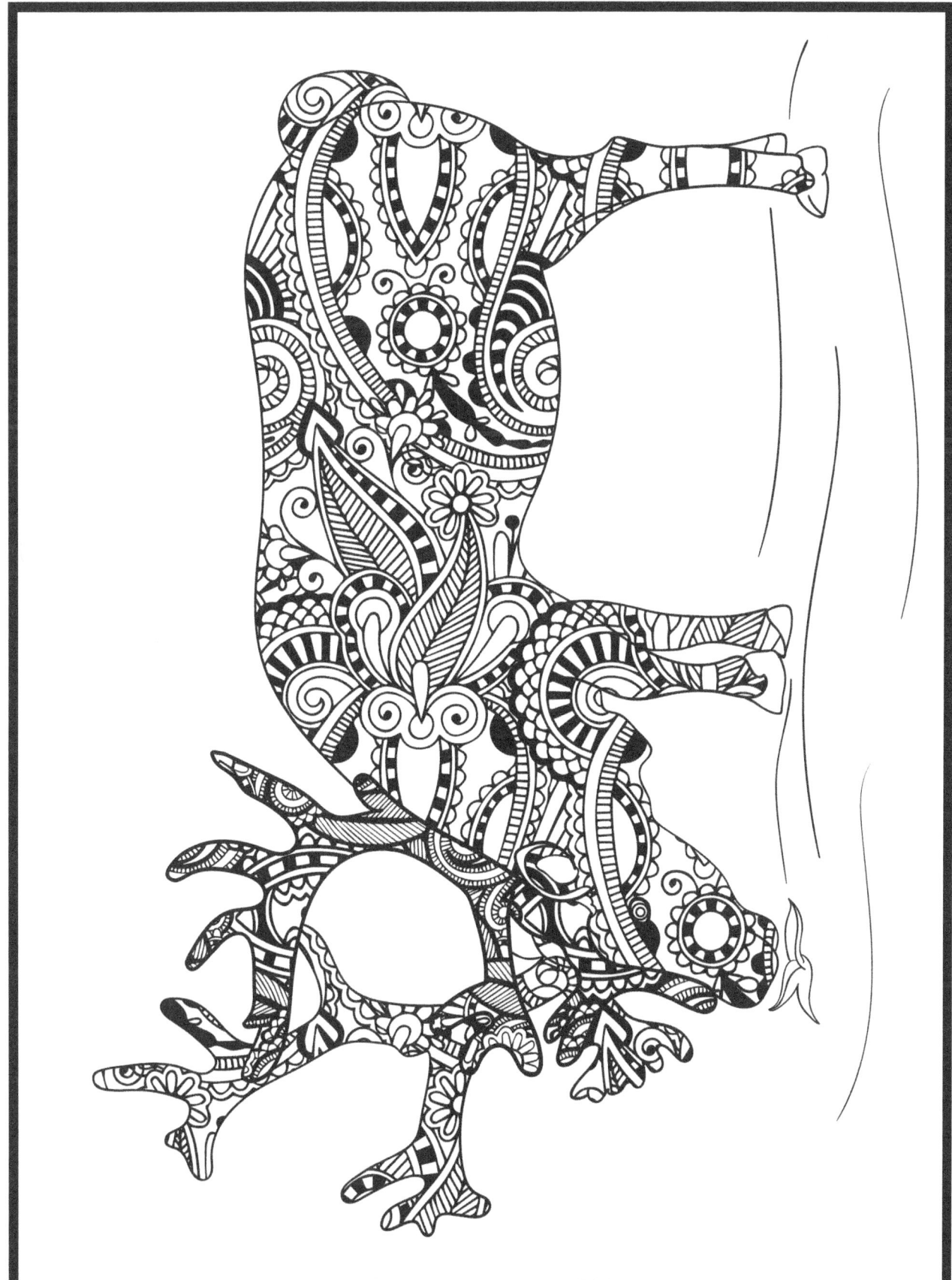

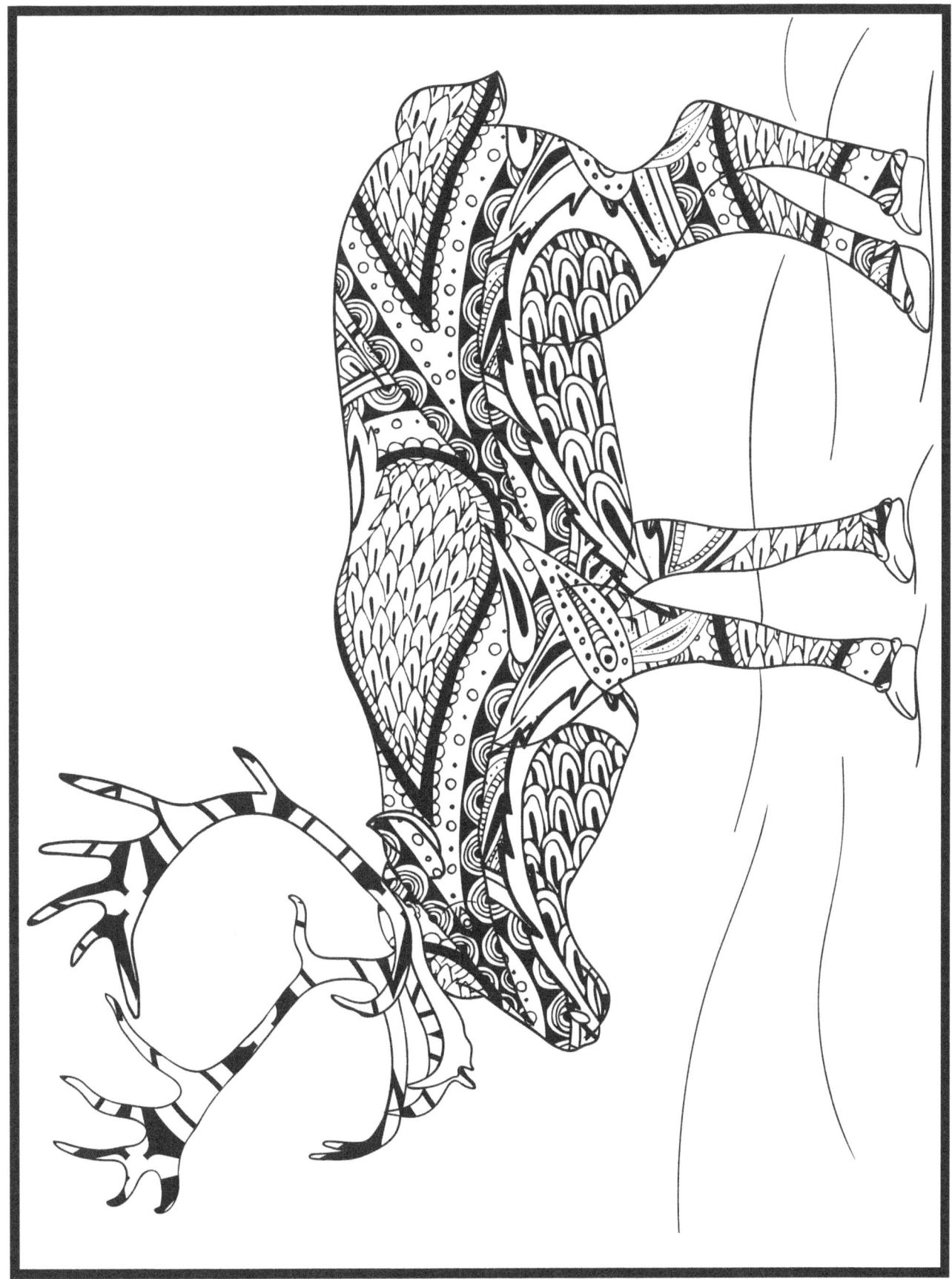

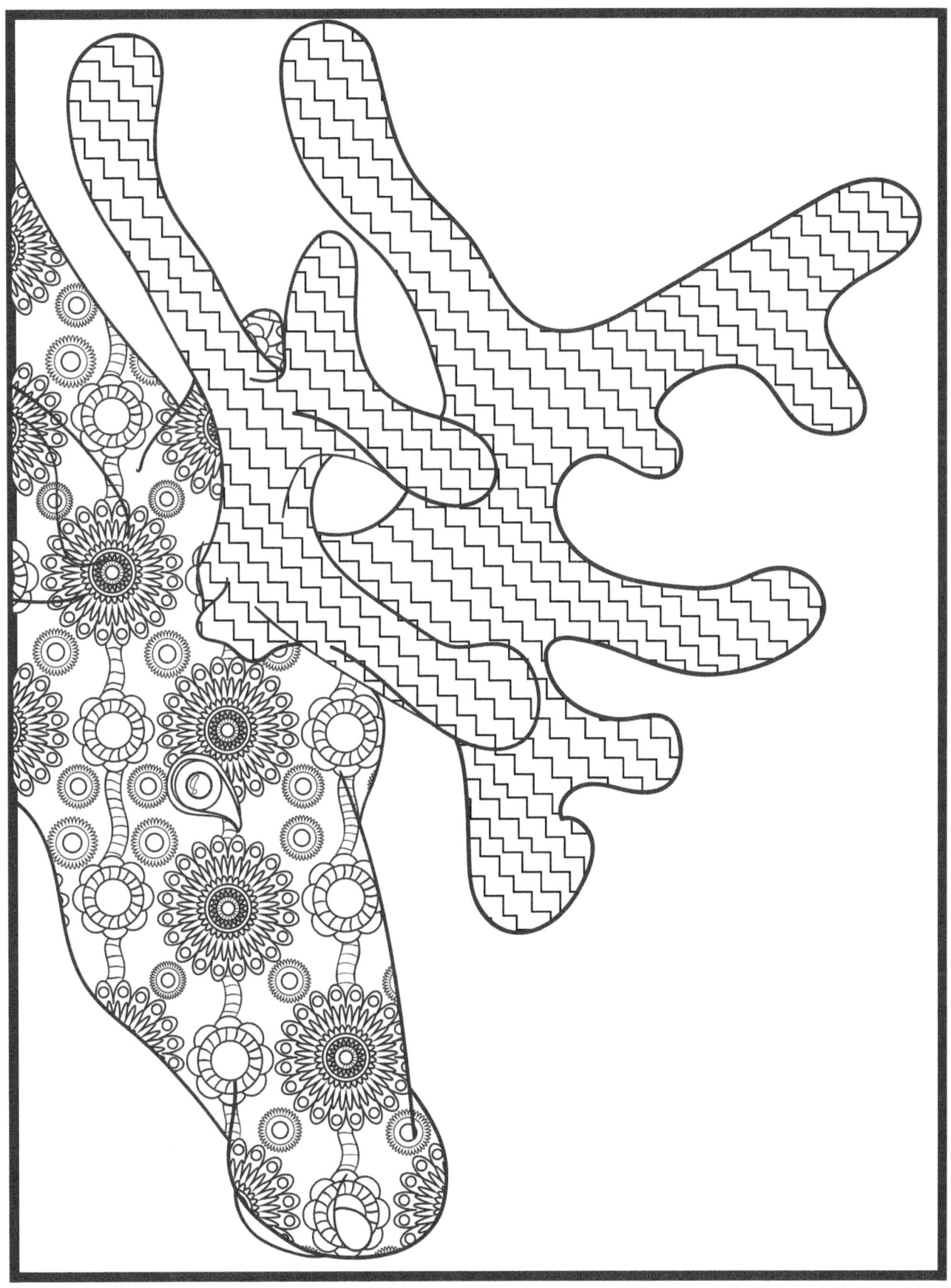

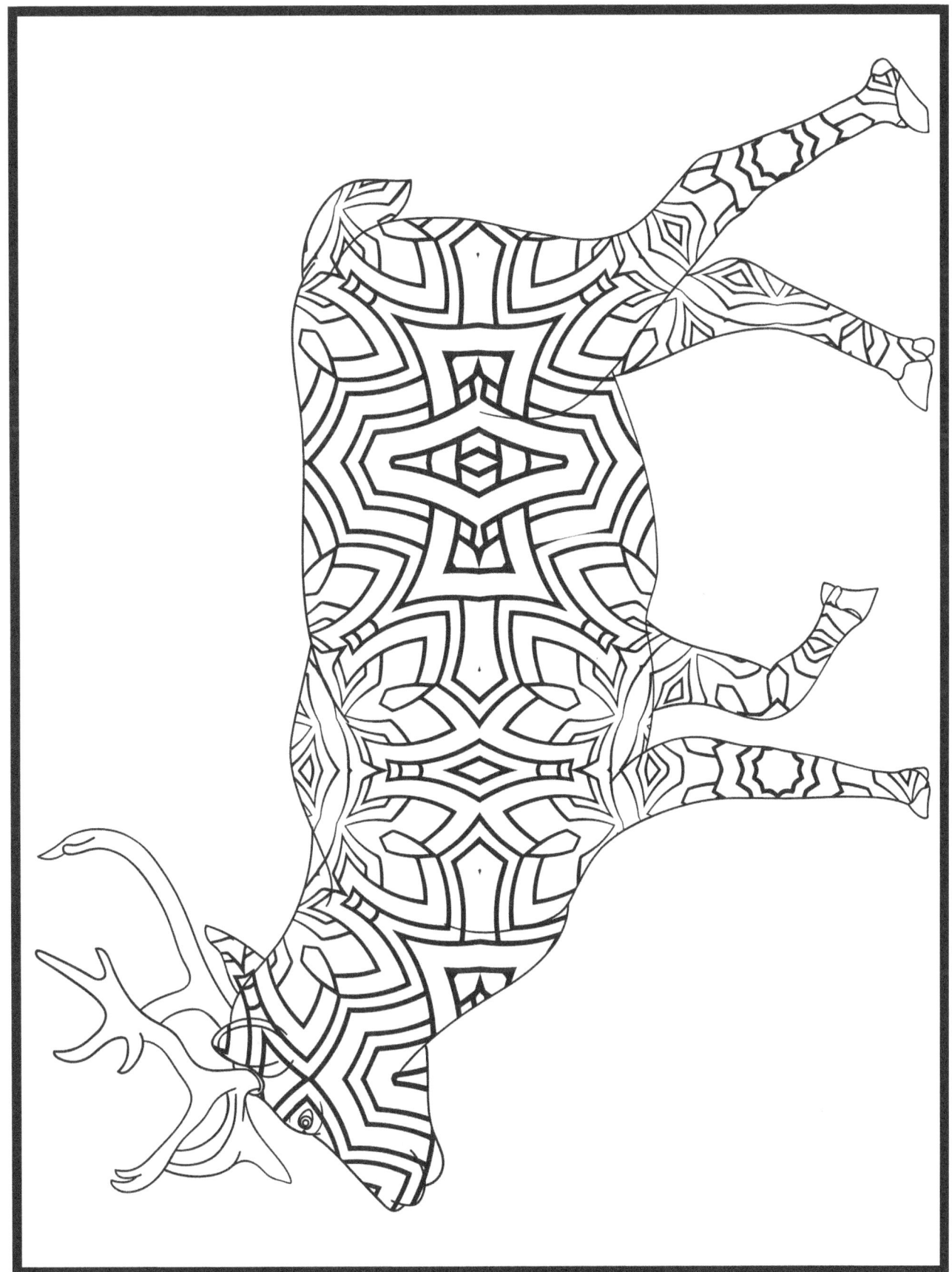

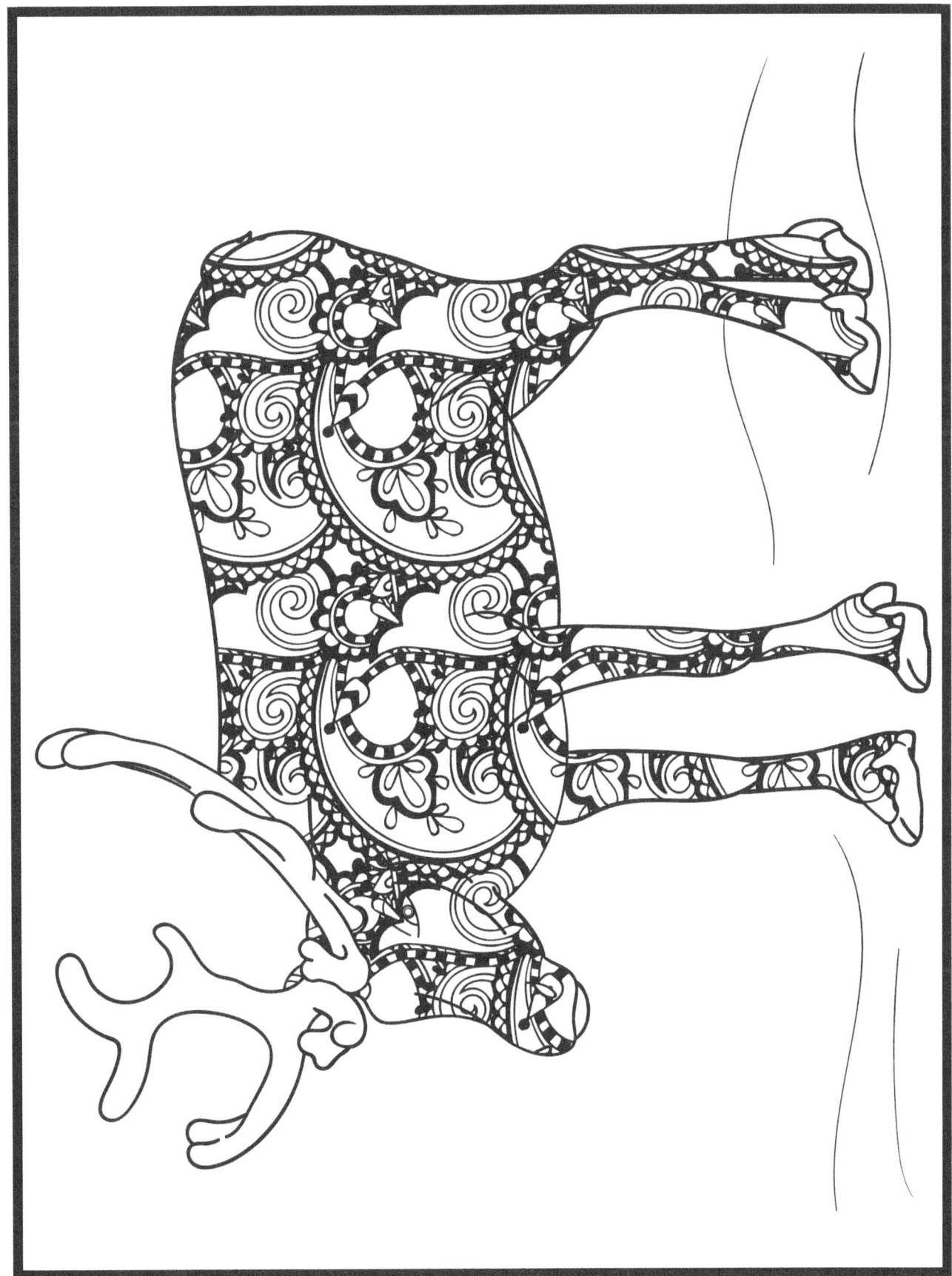

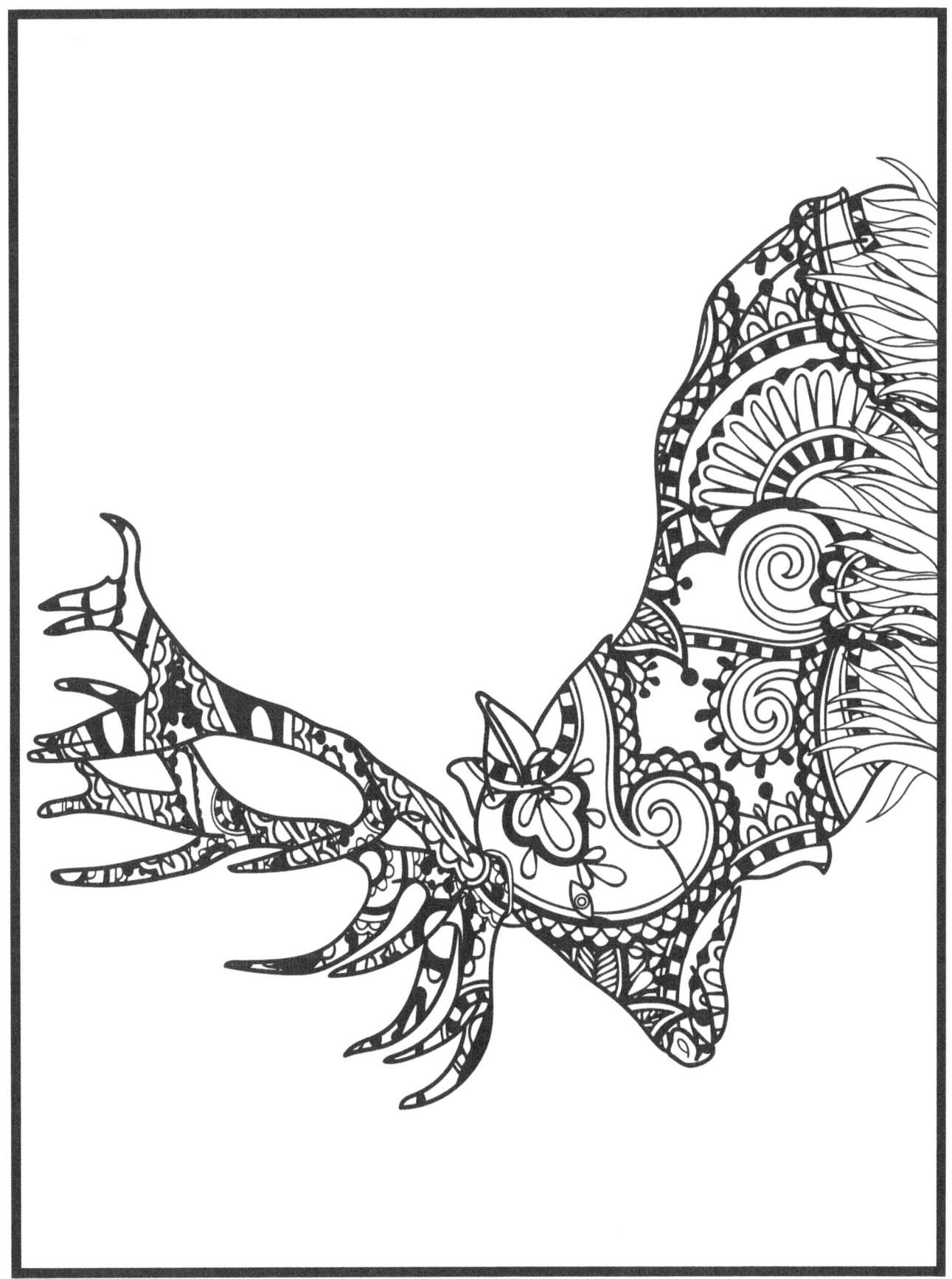

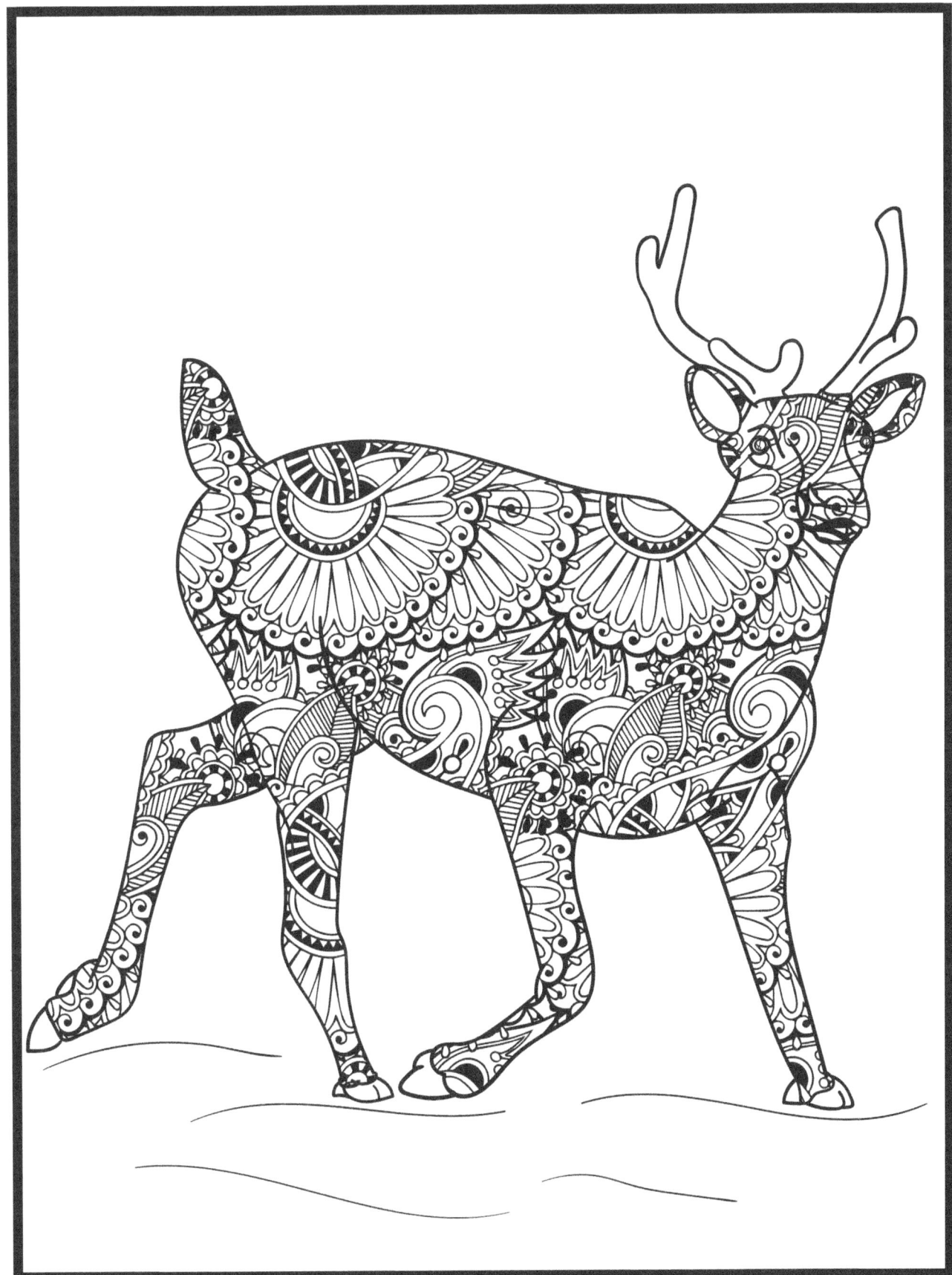

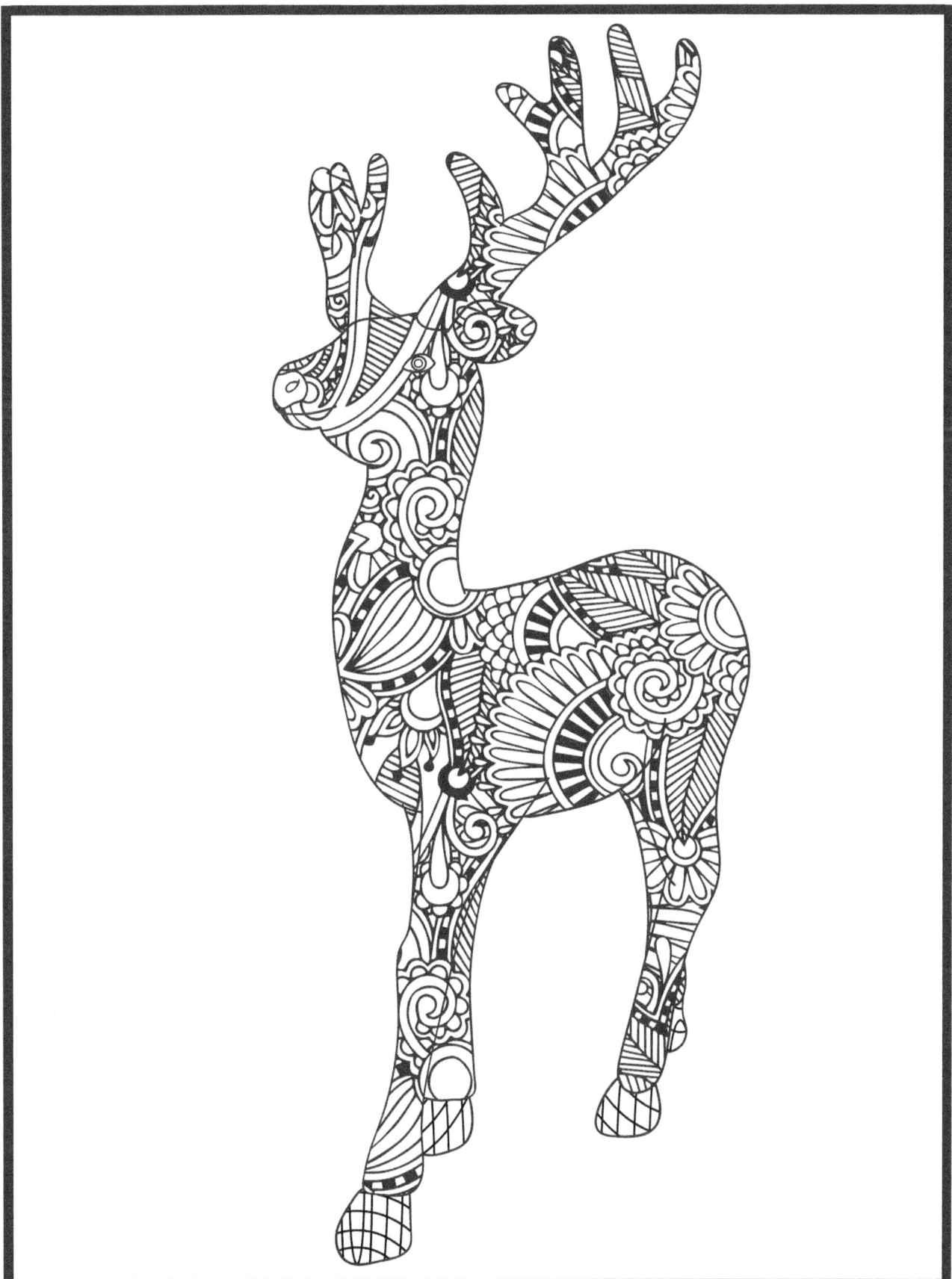

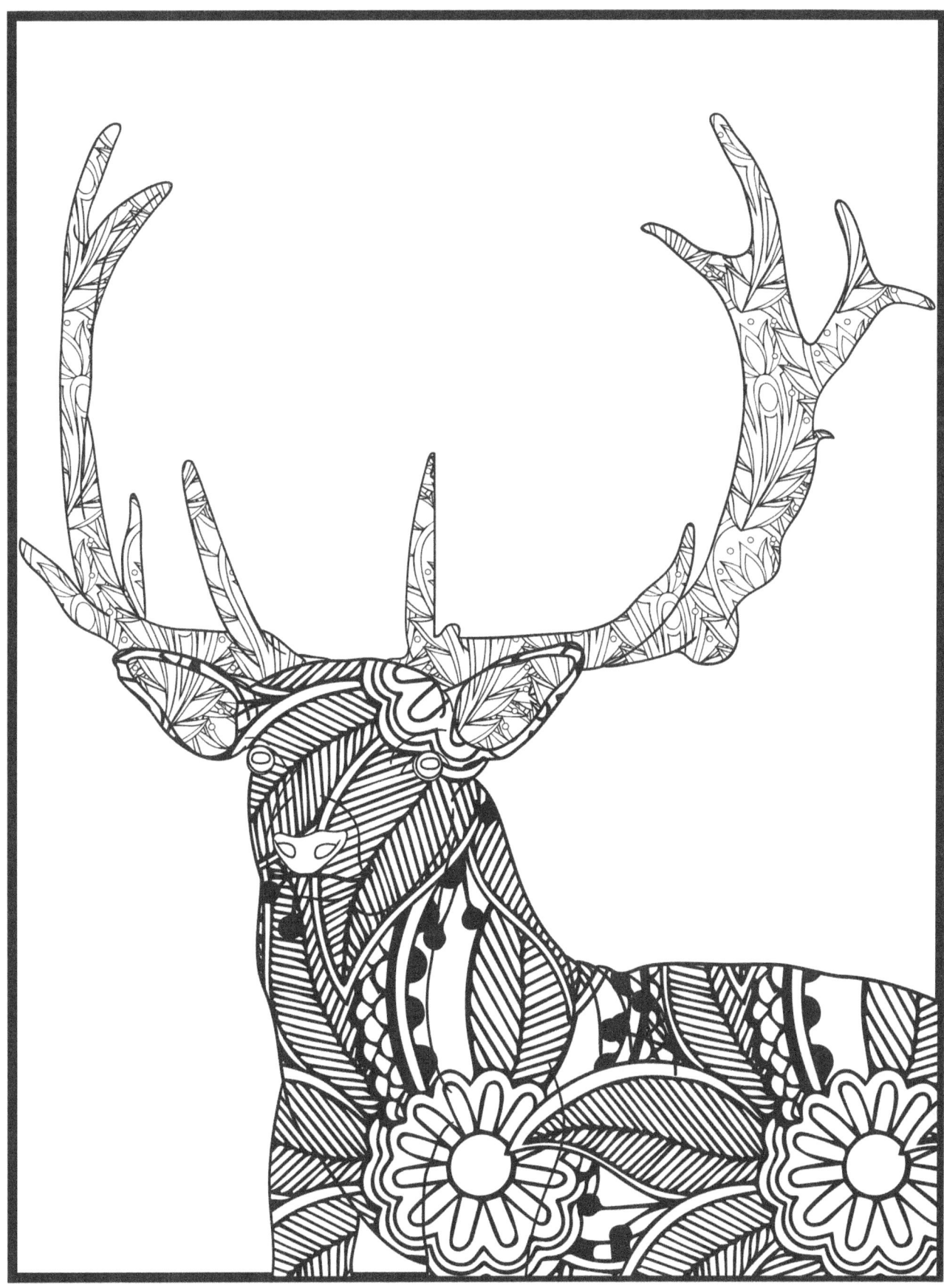

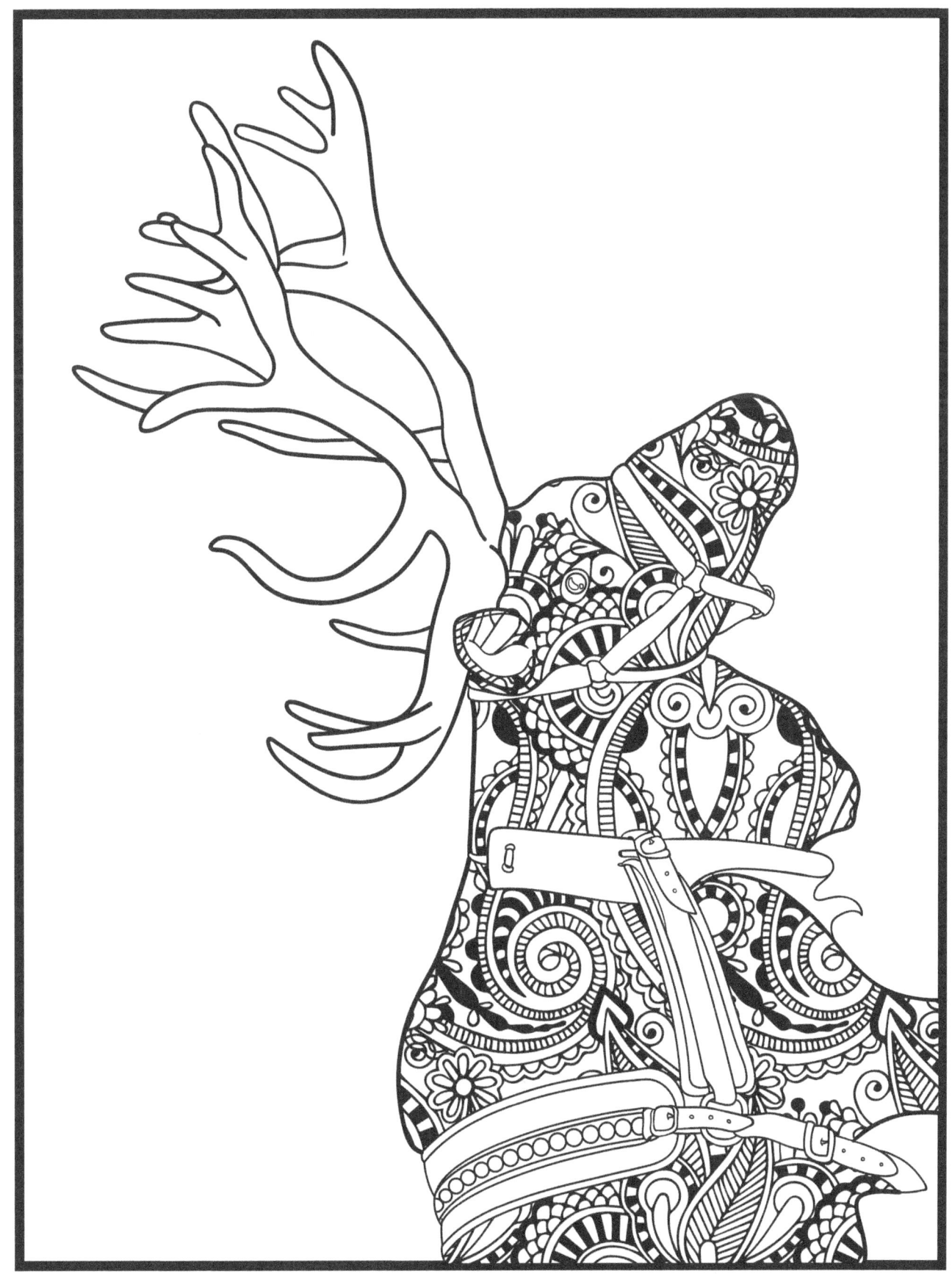

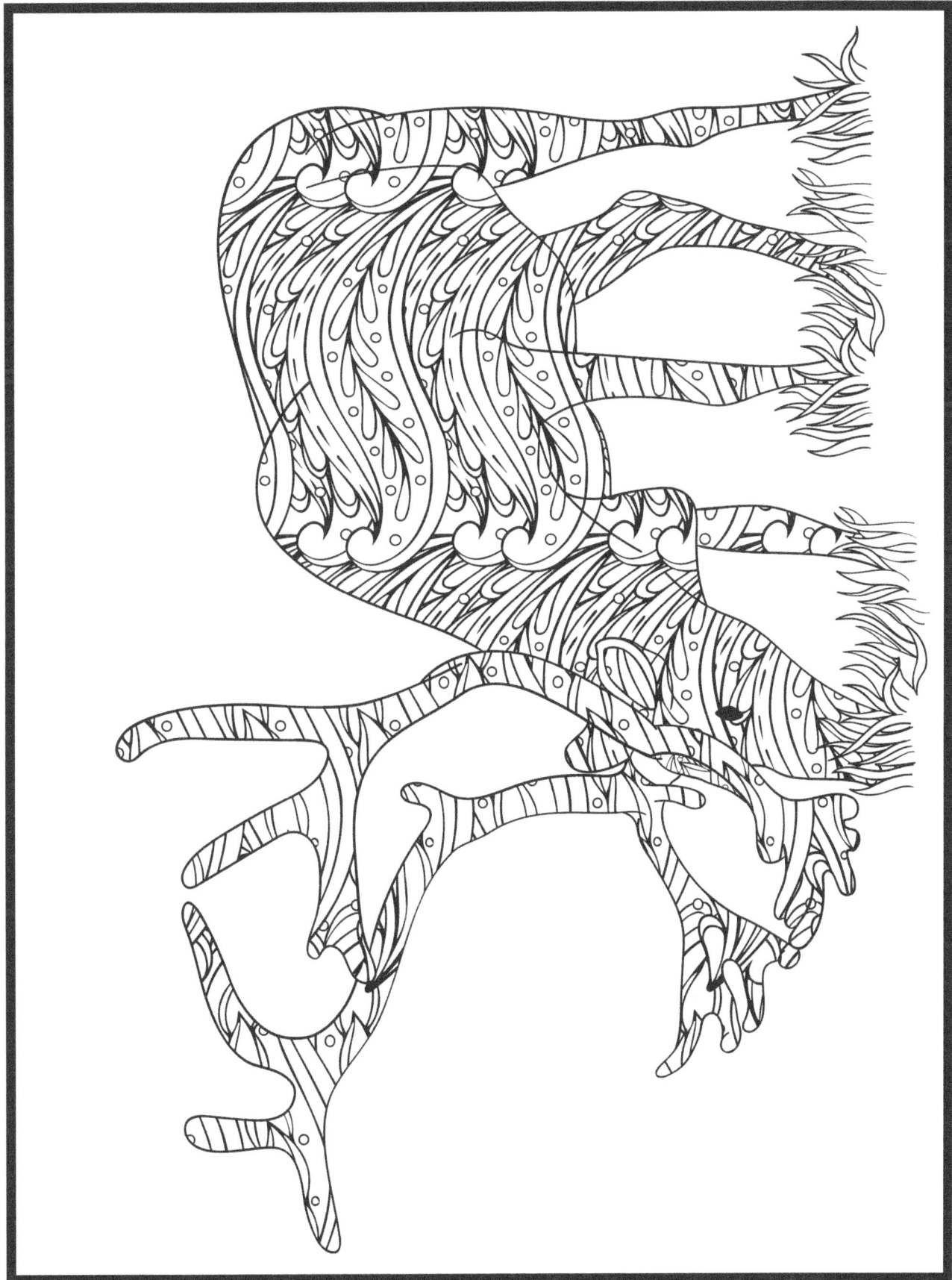

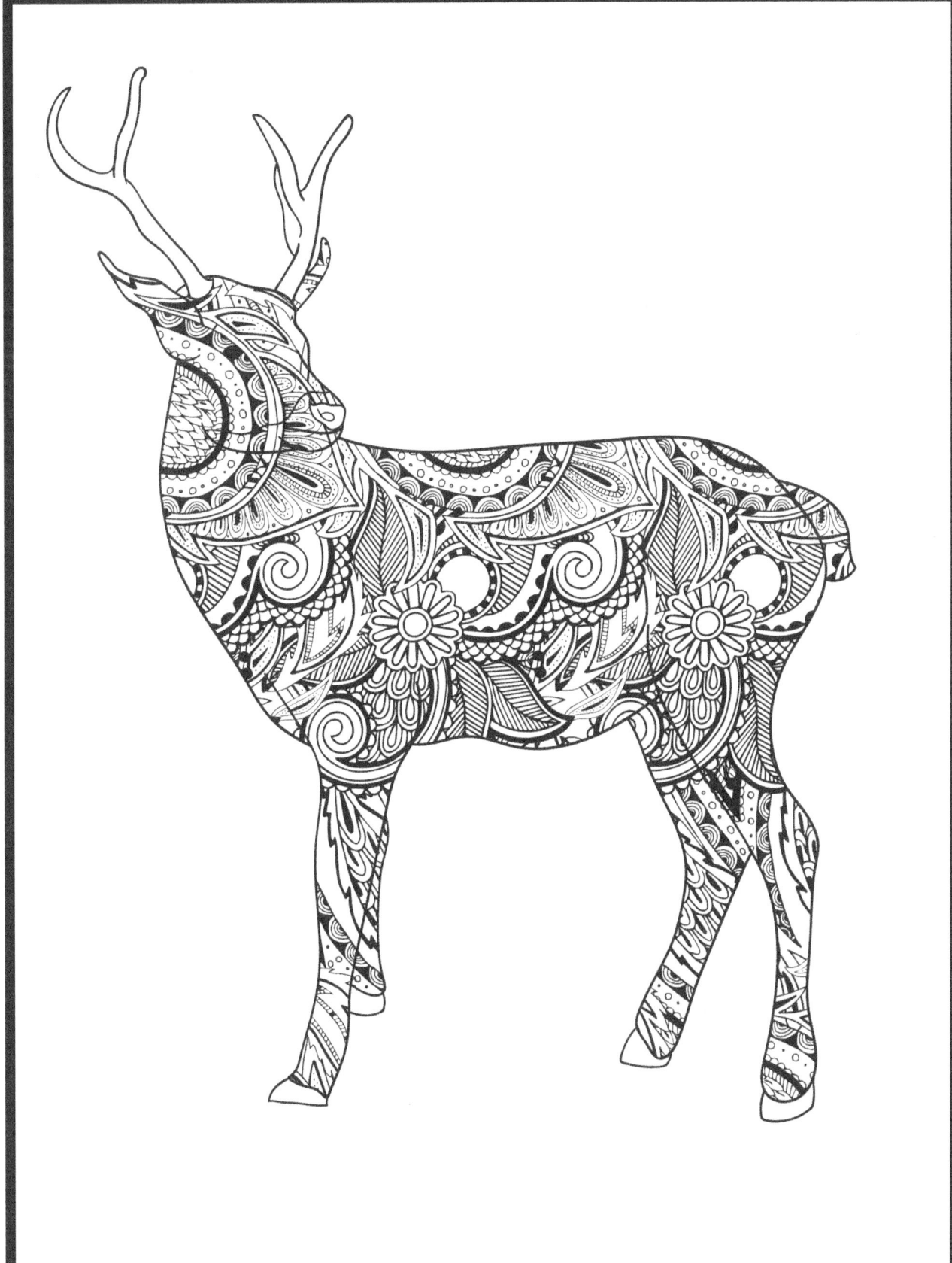

COLOR TEST PAGE

COLOR TEST PAGE